Layers of Learning
Year Four • Unit Eighteen

Civil Rights
Home State Study I
Instincts
Theater & Film

Published by HooDoo Publishing
United States of America
(Grilled Cheese BTN Font) © Fontdiner - www.fontdiner.com
ISBN #978-1974003648

Units at a Glance: Topics For All Four Years of the Layers of Learning Program

1	History	Geography	Science	The Arts
1	Mesopotamia	Maps & Globes	Planets	Cave Paintings
2	Egypt	Map Keys	Stars	Egyptian Art
3	Europe	Global Grids	Earth & Moon	Crafts
4	Ancient Greece	Wonders	Satellites	Greek Art
5	Babylon	Mapping People	Humans in Space	Poetry
6	The Levant	Physical Earth	Laws of Motion	List Poems
7	Phoenicians	Oceans	Motion	Moral Stories
8	Assyrians	Deserts	Fluids	Rhythm
9	Persians	Arctic	Waves	Melody
10	Ancient China	Forests	Machines	Chinese Art
11	Early Japan	Mountains	States of Matter	Line & Shape
12	Arabia	Rivers & Lakes	Atoms	Color & Value
13	Ancient India	Grasslands	Elements	Texture & Form
14	Ancient Africa	Africa	Bonding	African Tales
15	First North Americans	North America	Salts	Creative Kids
16	Ancient South America	South America	Plants	South American Art
17	Celts	Europe	Flowering Plants	Jewelry
18	Roman Republic	Asia	Trees	Roman Art
19	Christianity	Australia & Oceania	Simple Plants	Instruments
20	Roman Empire	You Explore	Fungi	Composing Music

2	History	Geography	Science	The Arts
1	Byzantines	Turkey	Climate & Seasons	Byzantine Art
2	Barbarians	Ireland	Forecasting	Illumination
3	Islam	Arabian Peninsula	Clouds & Precipitation	Creative Kids
4	Vikings	Norway	Special Effects	Viking Art
5	Anglo Saxons	Britain	Wild Weather	King Arthur Tales
6	Charlemagne	France	Cells & DNA	Carolingian Art
7	Normans	Nigeria	Skeletons	Canterbury Tales
8	Feudal System	Germany	Muscles, Skin, Cardio	Gothic Art
9	Crusades	Balkans	Digestive & Senses	Religious Art
10	Burgundy, Venice, Spain	Switzerland	Nerves	Oil Paints
11	Wars of the Roses	Russia	Health	Minstrels & Plays
12	Eastern Europe	Hungary	Metals	Printmaking
13	African Kingdoms	Mali	Carbon Chemistry	Textiles
14	Asian Kingdoms	Southeast Asia	Non-metals	Vivid Language
15	Mongols	Caucasus	Gases	Fun With Poetry
16	Medieval China & Japan	China	Electricity	Asian Arts
17	Pacific Peoples	Micronesia	Circuits	Arts of the Islands
18	American Peoples	Canada	Technology	Indian Legends
19	The Renaissance	Italy	Magnetism	Renaissance Art I
20	Explorers	Caribbean Sea	Motors	Renaissance Art II

www.Layers-of-Learning.com

3	History	Geography	Science	The Arts
1	Age of Exploration	Argentina & Chile	Classification & Insects	Fairy Tales
2	The Ottoman Empire	Egypt & Libya	Reptiles & Amphibians	Poetry
3	Mogul Empire	Pakistan & Afghanistan	Fish	Mogul Arts
4	Reformation	Angola & Zambia	Birds	Reformation Art
5	Renaissance England	Tanzania & Kenya	Mammals & Primates	Shakespeare
6	Thirty Years' War	Spain	Sound	Baroque Music
7	The Dutch	Netherlands	Light & Optics	Baroque Art I
8	France	Indonesia	Bending Light	Baroque Art II
9	The Enlightenment	Korean Peninsula	Color	Art Journaling
10	Russia & Prussia	Central Asia	History of Science	Watercolors
11	Conquistadors	Baltic States	Igneous Rocks	Creative Kids
12	Settlers	Peru & Bolivia	Sedimentary Rocks	Native American Art
13	13 Colonies	Central America	Metamorphic Rocks	Settler Sayings
14	Slave Trade	Brazil	Gems & Minerals	Colonial Art
15	The South Pacific	Australasia	Fossils	Principles of Art
16	The British in India	India	Chemical Reactions	Classical Music
17	The Boston Tea Party	Japan	Reversible Reactions	Folk Music
18	Founding Fathers	Iran	Compounds & Solutions	Rococo
19	Declaring Independence	Samoa & Tonga	Oxidation & Reduction	Creative Crafts I
20	The American Revolution	South Africa	Acids & Bases	Creative Crafts II

4	History	Geography	Science	The Arts
1	American Government	USA	Heat & Temperature	Patriotic Music
2	Expanding Nation	Pacific States	Motors & Engines	Tall Tales
3	Industrial Revolution	U.S. Landscapes	Energy	Romantic Art I
4	Revolutions	Mountain West States	Energy Sources	Romantic Art II
5	Africa	U.S. Political Maps	Energy Conversion	Impressionism I
6	The West	Southwest States	Earth Structure	Impressionism II
7	Civil War	National Parks	Plate Tectonics	Post Impressionism
8	World War I	Plains States	Earthquakes	Expressionism
9	Totalitarianism	U.S. Economics	Volcanoes	Abstract Art
10	Great Depression	Heartland States	Mountain Building	Kinds of Art
11	World War II	Symbols & Landmarks	Chemistry of Air & Water	War Art
12	Modern East Asia	The South	Food Chemistry	Modern Art
13	India's Independence	People of America	Industry	Pop Art
14	Israel	Appalachian States	Chemistry of Farming	Modern Music
15	Cold War	U.S. Territories	Chemistry of Medicine	Free Verse
16	Vietnam War	Atlantic States	Food Chains	Photography
17	Latin America	New England States	Animal Groups	Latin American Art
18	Civil Rights	Home State Study I	Instincts	Theater & Film
19	Technology	Home State Study II	Habitats	Architecture
20	Terrorism	America in Review	Conservation	Creative Kids

Unit 4-18

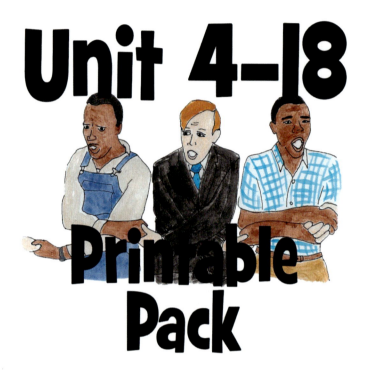

Printable Pack

This unit includes printables at the end. To make life easier for you we also created digital printable packs for each unit. To retrieve your printable pack for Unit 4-18, please visit

www.layers-of-learning.com/digital-printable-packs/

Put the printable pack in your shopping cart and use this coupon code:

718UNIT4-18

Your printable pack will be free.

Layers of Learning Introduction

This is part of a series of units in the Layers of Learning homeschool curriculum, including the subjects of history, geography, science, and the arts. Children from 1st through 12th can participate in the same curriculum at the same time - family school style.

The units are intended to be used in order as the basis of a complete curriculum (once you add in a systematic math, reading, and writing program). You begin with Year 1 Unit 1 no matter what ages your children are. Spend about 2 weeks on each unit. You pick and choose the activities within the unit that appeal to you and read the books from the book list that are available to you or find others on the same topic from your library. We highly recommend that you use the timeline in every history section as the backbone. Then flesh out your learning with reading and activities that highlight the topics you think are the most important.

Alternatively, you can use the units as activity ideas to supplement another curriculum in any order you wish. You can still use them with all ages of children at the same time.

When you've finished with Year One, move on to Year Two, Year Three, and Year Four. Then begin again with Year One and work your way through the years again. Now your children will be older, reading more involved books, and writing more in depth. When you have completed the sequence for the second time, you start again on it for the third and final time. If your student began with Layers of Learning in 1st grade and stayed with it all the way through she would go through the four year rotation three times, firmly cementing the information in her mind in ever increasing depth. At each level you should expect increasing amounts of outside reading and writing. High schoolers in particular should be reading extensively, and if possible, participating in discussion groups.

These icons will guide you in spotting activities and books that are appropriate for the age of child you are working with. But if you think an activity is too juvenile or too difficult for your kids, adjust accordingly. The icons are not there as rules, just guides.

☺ 1st-4th
☺ 5th-8th
☺ 9th-12th

Within each unit we share:

EXPLORATIONS, activities relating to the topic;
EXPERIMENTS, usually associated with science topics;
EXPEDITIONS, field trips;
EXPLANATIONS, teacher helps or educational philosophies.

In the sidebars we also include Additional Layers, Famous Folks, Fabulous Facts, On the Web, and other extra related topics that can take you off on tangents, exploring the world and your interests with a bit more freedom. The curriculum will always be there to pull you back on track when you're ready.

UNIT EIGHTEEN

CIVIL RIGHTS - HOME STATE STUDY I - INSTINCTS - THEATER & FILM

Darkness cannot drive out darkness; only light can do that. Hate cannot drive out hate; only love can do that.
-Martin Luther King Jr.

LIBRARY LIST

<table>
<tr><td rowspan="1">HISTORY</td><td>Search for: civil rights, women's rights, suffrage, racism, apartheid, human rights

😊 <u>Harvesting Hope: The Story of Cesar Chavez</u> by Kathleen Krull. Chavez led a movement for better conditions and pay for migrant workers in California.

😊 <u>If You Lived When Women Won Their Rights</u> by Anne Kamma.

😊 <u>Whoever You Are</u> by Mem Fox. Promotes the idea that people are different and all are valuable.

😊 😊 <u>Separate is Never Equal</u> by Duncan Tonatiuh. Tells the story of segregated schools in California and the Mexican-American family who changed that.

😊 😊 <u>Malala Yousafzai: Warrior with Words</u> by Karen Leggett Abouraya. True story of a teenage girl who was shot by the Taliban because she wanted an education. May be too disturbing for young children, pre-read.

😊 😊 <u>We Are All Born Free: The Universal Declaration of Human Rights in Pictures</u> by Amnesty International. Discuss these rights one by one with your kids.

😊 <u>The Civil Rights Movement</u> by Heather Adamson. This is a choose-your-own-adventure style book that takes place in real history about the U.S. civil rights movement.

😊 <u>Esperanza Rising</u> by Pam Muñoz Ryan. Fictional story of a well-to-do girl who emigrates from Mexico and ends up working as a migrant worker in California.

😊 <u>You Want Women to Vote, Lizzie Stanton?</u> by Jean Fritz.

😊 😊 <u>Waiting for the Rain</u> by Sheila Gordon. Two boys, one black and one white, grow up as friends in South Africa, but they soon learn their friendship is unacceptable. What will they do?

😊 😊 <u>Freedom's Children: Young Civil Rights Activists Tell Their Own Stories</u> by Ellen S. Levine. Focuses on the contributions of young people during the civil rights movement of the 1950s and 1960s in the United States.

😊 😊 <u>With Courage and Cloth: Winning the Fight for a Woman's Right to Vote</u> by Ann Bausum.

😊 <u>Civil Rights: Rhetoric or Reality</u> by Thomas Sowell. Written in the 1980s, this book discusses the things that went right and the things that went wrong in the aftermath of the civil rights movement of the United States. Sowell is a celebrated intellectual, but he writes in an easy to understand style in this short book.

😊 <u>Kaffir Boy: The True Story of a Black Youth's Coming of Age in Apartheid South Africa</u> by Mark Mathabane. An autobiography of the author's childhood and escape from discrimination and poverty.</td></tr>
</table>

GEOGRAPHY	Search for: your state ☺ ☻ ☻ Rand McNally State Map (for your state) ☺ ☻ ☻ Moon Handbook (for your state). Gives travel, vacation, and destination ideas. ☺ My First Book About . . . by Carole Marsh. Fill in your state. ☺ ☻ What's Great About . . . ? (Our Great States series). ☺ ☻ The Incredible Idaho Coloring Book by Carole Marsh. Only, look for your state of course. ☺ ☻ . . . Interactive Notebook by Carole Marsh. Again, look for your state.
SCIENCE	Search for: instincts, migration, hibernation, camouflage ☺ How To Hide A Meadow Frog and Other Amphibians by Ruth Heller. ☺ How Polar Animals Hide by Melvin and Gilda Berger. ☻ Becoming Invisible: From Camouflage to Cloaks by Carla Mooney. ☺ Over and Under the Snow by Kate Messner. ☺ Hibernation by Margaret Hall. ☺ They Just Know: Animal Instincts by Robin Yardi. ☺ Great Migrations: Amazing Animal Journeys by Laura Marsh. ☺ Great Migrations: Whales by Laura Marsh. Look for other animal migrations in this series from National Geographic. ☺ Animals in Winter by Henrietta Bancroft. Talks about migration and hibernation. ☺ ☻ The Journey: Stories of Migration by Cynthia Rylant. ☻ Wildlife Spectacles: Mass Migrations, Mating Rituals, and Other Fascinating Animal Behaviors by Vladimir Dinets. Filled with pictures and the first hand experiences with the author in observing animals.
THE ARTS	Search for: theater, plays, film, movies, making movies, film industry, specific actor/director biographies. If you are interested in either listening to or a performing a reader's theater rather than a full-scale production, you can find lots of reader's theater resources as well. ☺ ☻ Theater for Young Audiences: 20 Great Plays for Children by Coleman A. Jennings and Maurice Sendak. ☺ ☻ Theater Shoes by Elizabeth Sastre. This is a novel about some orphan children during World War II who go to a school of stage theater. It would make a fun read aloud during this unit. ☺ ☻ ☻ Theater Games for Young Performers: Improvisations and Exercises for Developing Acting Skills by Maria C. Novelly. This books lists lots of games and ideas for fun ways to teach kids to be actors. There are also some worksheets included. ☻ ☻ The Film Encyclopedia 7th Edition: The Complete Guide to Film and the Film Industry by Ephraim Katz and Ronald Dean Nolen. ☺ Film History: An Introduction by Kristen Thompson and David Bordwell. This is a worldwide look at the film industry and its history. ☻ Film Directing Shot by Shot: Visualizing from Concept to Screen by Steven D. Katz. This is a book about how to tell stories while directing a film.

History: Civil Rights

Fabulous Fact

Though the idea of rights for all people has existed for a long time, the modern philosophy didn't emerge until the second half of the 20th century when totalitarian states were on the rise. The well-broadcasted horrors inflicted on citizens all over the world caused the movement to restore human dignity and happiness.

Additional Layer

Even though slavery is illegal all over the world, it still exists in many forms, even in first world countries. It's just done in secret now. Read: https://www.theatlantic.com/magazine/archive/2017/06/lolas-story/524490/

On the Web

Watch "What are the Universal Human Rights" from TED-Ed: https://youtu.be/nDgIVseTkuE. The video talks about different types of rights, the UN Universal Declaration of Human Rights, and why human rights abuses are still happening. Discuss the video with your kids.

Civil rights are rights recognized by governments. Usually they are protected by law and prevent the government from abusing citizens or treating citizens differently from one another based on externalities like class, race, gender, religion, or geographic location.

The idea that citizens should have protected rights began with the Anglo-Saxons, who had written laws preventing the government from abusing citizens. For example, men in Anglo-Saxon England could be called upon to defend the nation. This was obligatory. But by law they could only be called up if the Wittengamot, the king's council, agreed, and then only for a maximum of four months at a time. This protected the farmers and landholders from sending their farms and businesses into ruin when the government waged political wars. They also had rights that allowed them a fair trial and prevented the government from taking their land or homes. The English lost all these rights at the time of the Norman invasion, but they were slowly restored from the time the nobles forced King John to sign the Magna Carta in 1215. By the time the English were making colonies in North America, the idea that Englishmen had rights that could not be infringed on by government was very well entrenched. It was because England was treading on these rights that the Americans revolted in 1775.

Civil rights were then written into the Constitution of the

This is Eleanor Roosevelt holding up a copy of the Universal Declaration of Human Rights, which was crafted in 1948 after the horrors of WWII.

United States in the form of the Bill of Rights. After that landmark document was written, nations around the world began to reform their governments after the model of a republic and they included written documents that explained what rights a citizen of their country could expect. This was the beginning of the modern civil rights movement.

Of course, there were and still are many injustices and offenses to the rights of people by their governments across the world, including in the nations that first championed the rights of mankind. We'll learn about some of them below.

☺ ☻ ☻ EXPLORATION: Timeline
You will find printable timeline squares at the end of this unit. This timeline covers civil rights across the world and is rather general. You may want to delve more deeply into civil rights issues that hit closer to home. You can assign your kids to create a more detailed timeline of the women's vote or the black civil rights movement in the United States or another topic.

Place the timeline squares on a wall timeline or in a notebook timeline. Timelines work best when used alongside timelines from other units so you can see events around the world at the same time in history.

☻ ☻ EXPLORATION: Types of Rights
There are three major categories of rights that are recognized.

1. Civil rights
2. Political rights
3. Social rights

Civil rights include the right to be treated fairly by your government and protect the life, liberty, and property of the individual from abuse by their government. They include things like the right to a fair trial, the right to give testimony and receive counsel in court, the right to own property, the right to speak freely, the right to worship as your conscience sees fit, and the right to be treated by your government in the same manner as every other citizen.

Political rights include things like the right to vote, to run for office, or to serve on a jury. If you don't have these rights it doesn't destroy your life, liberty, or property, but it does mean you have no say in the way your government is run.

The last class of rights are social rights. These rights govern the way people treat each other in private life, and they define what

Additional Layer

In Britain Catholics had been discriminated against since Henry VIII. Catholics were imprisoned, had property confiscated, were denied the vote and the right to sit in parliament, and other violations of rights.

The Roman Catholic Relief Act of 1829 finally ended the persecution.

Photo by Quodvultdeus, CC by SA 3.0 Wikimedia

Priest holes, like the one above, were built into many private homes in England when being Catholic was a crime. A priest could hide behind the walls or escape out a tunnel while a search was being carried out.

Additional Layer

Though there are international "laws" protecting human rights, they are unenforceable. Instead, public opinion and political pressure are used to convince governments to protect people. Amnesty International is a private group that works to provide this pressure.

Famous Folks

Cesar Chavez was a civil rights leader in California in the 1960s through the 1980s. He saw that migrant workers had terrible wages, housing, educational opportunities, and access to healthcare.

He worked to form unions for the farm workers. Learn more about him.

Writer's Workshop

Negative rights require the individual to act in order to benefit from the right. If you want an education, *you* must go and get it.

There is an argument about whether it is fair or realistic to expect people to meet their own needs. What do you think it does to the human spirit to be handed things or to have to go and figure out how to get it for yourself?

Is it kind to provide food, housing, education, and so on, or not?

Write about your ideas.

people deserve to have as human beings. They say you can't decide who to serve and who not to serve in your private business. They say that everyone deserves healthcare and housing and a job. These rights require someone to do something, or at least to put aside their own belief systems to comply with them. If you have a right to be served in my restaurant, then I must serve you in my restaurant no matter what I think of you personally. If you have a right to a job, then I must provide you with a job whether or not you benefit me in some way and whether or not I can afford to pay you.

At the end of this unit you will find matching cards. The three headings are "Civil Rights," "Political Rights," and "Social Rights." Below these three heading cards are specific rights that have been claimed by people in various times and places. The rights are placed under the correct heading before they are cut apart so the parent can use that as a key. After you cut them apart, determine to which category each of these rights belong, and place them under the correct heading. Not everyone agrees about which rights ought to be enforced by law. Discuss which of these rights you think are valid and which are not and why.

☺ EXPLORATION: Negative and Positive Rights

Governments can phrase the written rights of their citizens in two ways. A right can be written as a negative right, where the government is told it "shall not infringe" on certain rights which are understood to be held by the people under natural law. These rights are often considered inalienable rights, or those which cannot be taken away.

The other way governments can phrase rights is as positive rights, where the government tells the people which rights it is granting them. These rights would be written like "the people have the right to assemble."

Think about the difference between the belief that rights are natural and the belief that rights are granted by governments. Which philosophy do you think is true? Where do rights come from? What does your religious philosophy teach about human rights? What is the worth of a person, and what is government's role in defending the worth of a person?

Read the United States Bill of Rights, the first ten amendments, and determine whether these are negative rights or positive rights. You can find the Bill of Rights online here: http://www.archives. gov/exhibits/charters/bill_of_rights_transcript.html

Then read the UN Universal Declaration of Human Rights. Are

these rights written as positive or negative rights? You can find the UN declaration here: http://www.un.org/en/documents/udhr/.

Another meaning of a positive right is where a government expects someone to act. For example, if someone has the right to healthcare, then someone else is obliged to provide that healthcare with or without remuneration. Look back through the two documents. Are there any rights listed that require someone to act so the right can be met? What do you think about this sort of right? Would these sorts of rights be natural rights or rights imposed by government?

☺ ☺ ☺ **EXPLORATION: Abolition in the United States**
American abolitionist movements had been vibrant since before the Revolutionary War, but strong opposition in the South meant that in order to preserve the union of the states, the issue of slavery had to be put off. It continued to be put off until the 1850s when violence, and then war, broke out between the states who wanted abolition and the states who wanted to preserve slavery. The free states won, and in 1865 slavery was abolished in America. Read the 13th Amendment to the Constitution for yourself: http://www.ourdocuments.gov/doc.php?doc=40 .

You can see the actual document and read the transcript at the above site. Take time to read the background behind the amendment on the same page. After you read, make this craft to help your kids remember the 13th Amendment.

Craft a number 13 from tissue paper, glue and a sheet of paper. Cut tissue paper into little 2" x 2" squares. Wrap the tissue paper squares around the eraser end of a pencil, and then stick them down on the sheet of paper with glue inside the outline of the number 13.

Famous Folks

William Lloyd Garrison was an abolitionist newspaper publisher and writer from Boston, Massachusetts. He became the center of the abolitionist movement in the United States in the years before the Civil War.

Interestingly, his experiences working for abolition convinced him that women, who were much more likely than men to oppose slavery and work for its end than men, should have a political voice.

Memorization Station

Kids can memorize section 1 of the 13th Amendment.

Neither slavery nor involuntary servitude, except as a punishment for crime whereof the party shall have been duly convicted, shall exist within the United States, or any place subject to their jurisdiction.

Additional Layer

What we said about political rights of women applies just as much to the rights of other groups: blacks in America, Catholics in England, Jews in Europe, children, and so on.

Famous Folks

Elizabeth Blackwell was the first female doctor in the United States and the first to be registered in Great Britain.

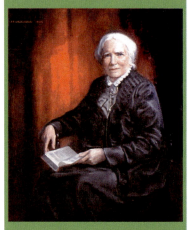

Reading a biography about her life will help your kids understand the struggles that women (and other discriminated against groups) had that men never did.

We like the biography, *The First Woman Doctor* by Rachel Baker and Evelyn Copelman.

Read it aloud together during this unit so you can discuss the ideas in the book together.

☺ ☺ ☺ EXPLORATION: Women's Rights

Before the 1900s very few women had any political rights. They couldn't vote or run for office. Women didn't serve on juries. In many cases the lack of political rights meant that women's civil rights were unprotected as well. Often women could not bring a suit to a court of law, testify in a trial, own property, have custody of their children in case of death or divorce, or attend universities (even if they had the money). Sometimes women lost even the right to not be abused or mistreated by their husbands or other men. Political rights tend to be necessary to protect civil rights. People with no political power have no means of forcing their government to protect their life, liberty, or property.

After you have read a bit more about the women's movement, have a discussion about voting rights. Why do you think men were able to vote, but women weren't? Did all men have the legal right to vote in 1850? Why was the vote restricted? Can everyone vote today? Why or why not? What factors should make a person eligible to vote?

When women marched in parades or protests, they often wore sashes across their bodies to show what they were marching for. The sashes usually said "Votes For Women." Make your own sash. You will need two wide pieces of ribbon. Glue the narrower onto the wider and write "Votes For Women" with a marker.

☺ ☺ EXPLORATION: Kate Shepherd's Ten Reasons

Kate Shepherd was born in Scotland and emigrated to New Zealand as a young woman. She became involved in the local temperance league and then began to work for the women's right to vote. She was very influential all over the world as a leader of women's suffrage.

She wrote a pamphlet in 1888 called "Ten Reasons Why the Women of New Zealand Should Vote." You can read it here: https://nzhistory.govt.nz/media/photo/ten-reasons-for-vote.

Write your own pamphlet called "Ten Reasons Why All People Should Vote." Fold a piece of paper into thirds. You can use Kate's ideas to give you inspiration for your ten reasons.

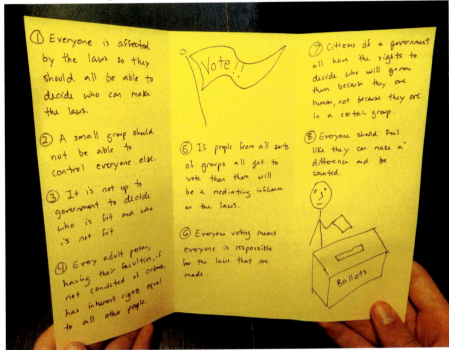

Famous Folks

Emmeline Pankhurst and her daughters, Crystabel and Sylvia, were essential to the suffragist movement in the UK. Learn more about who they were and what they did.

☺ ☻ **EXPLORATION: U.S. Civil Rights Movement Goals**

In the United States black people were (and sometimes are) subject to different laws and treated differently than white people. This started when slavery was introduced during colonial times. It continued even after slavery ended and constitutional amendments were passed to ensure equal protection of the law.

In the southern United States, where most black Americans lived at the time, the lines separating the races were the most defined. Black people drank from different water fountains, lived in different neighborhoods, went to different schools, worked and shopped at different places of business, and had to ride in the back of the bus. This different treatment was codified by law, and a black person who did not comply could be arrested or fined. The laws were known as Jim Crow Laws. The schools, neighborhoods, parks, and water fountains allowed to black people were not as nice as those provided for the whites. The southerners said the facilities and resources for the blacks were "separate but equal," but they weren't equal.

The goal of the Civil Rights Movement was to erase these lines of separation. The "I Have A Dream" speech which Martin Luther King Jr. delivered at the Lincoln Memorial in August of 1963 explains this overriding goal very well. Watch the speech: http://

Additional Layer

Men have had to fight for the right to vote too. Poor men, men without land, and men belonging to minority groups have all been denied the right to vote in many places.

On the Web

"Women's Suffrage Around the World" talks about the history of women gaining the vote. Watch it on YouTube: https://youtu.be/v3D-8f57vrN8.

Some of the places the video talks about are one-party or monarchies.

Writer's Workshop

Get several books, at your reading comprehension level, about Martin Luther King Jr. from the library. Read them, then write a biography of his life. Include a few facts about his youth and education then more details about his work toward civil and political rights for blacks in America. Little kids can narrate while their parent writes for them. Middle grades students should write about 1 ½ - 2 pages. High schoolers should write 3 or more pages.

On the Web

Get a printable timeline of the American black civil rights movement: http://www.layers-of-learning.com/civil-rights-movement-timeline/.

Famous Folks

Sir Douglas Nicholls worked his whole life to help his people, the Aborigines of Australia who had lost their way of life and then been discriminated against by their new government. Learn more about him.

youtu.be/HRIF4_WzU1w.

As you listen to the speech, write down the goals Martin Luther King Jr. talks about. Scatter the goals across your page, leaving room between them. Some of the goals can be met with the law and others require people to change their hearts. You can legislate and enforce "justice," but not "brotherhood." Draw a law tablet around the goals that can be met with the law. Draw a heart around the goals that require people to change their hearts.

Generally speaking, the goals that could be met with changes or enforcement of the law were met by the end of the 1960s. Do you think the goals that depend on individual attitudes have changed? Has there been progress made?

☺ ☺ ☺ **EXPLORATION: Martin Luther King Jr.**
Read a book or two about Martin Luther King Jr., and then draw a portrait of him in the middle of a piece of paper. You can use this simple tutorial: http://artprojectsforkids.org/how-draw-martin-luther-king/. Color the picture.

Find a quote from Martin Luther King Jr. that you like or that you think explains what his goals were. Write the quote on the bottom of the page.

You can do this same activity with other civil rights activists from this time period. Here are some people to consider who, like Martin Luther King Jr, impacted civil rights: Rosa Parks, Medgar Evars, Ruby Bridges, W.E.B. DuBois, and Willa Brown.

☺ ☺ ☺ **EXPLORATION: Apartheid and Nelson Mandela**
Apartheid was the legal segregation and discrimination against blacks in South Africa from 1948 to 1991, though the roots of it stretch back further. It was illegal for blacks to travel without a pass, work anywhere but in certain jobs, marry a white person, live anywhere but in designated black neighborhoods, or use the same public facilities as whites. They could not vote, speak freely, or run for political office.

People all over the world worked to end apartheid. One of those people was Nelson Mandela. Learn more about his life. There is a video biography in the sidebar. We also like *Nelson Mandela* by Lenny Hort and Laaren Brown. Search your library.

Make a bunting of Nelson Mandela. Write the letters of his name on triangular-shaped papers. Write a fact or a quote on each triangular piece and then color the pieces. Punch two holes in each piece of the bunting and thread a string through. Hang it on your wall to remember the fight for freedom in South Africa.

☺ ☺ ☺ EXPLORATION: Malala Yousafzai

Malala Yousafzai is a girl from Pakistan. Where she lives girls have been denied basic rights like education. Radical groups like the Taliban made laws that no girls were to attend school. They destroyed schools and terrorized people. Malala began to write and speak out on educational rights for girls when she was only eleven years old. Malala knew it was dangerous to speak out against the Taliban. She often heard shots fired at night, had to flee from her home, and received death threats. She spoke out anyway.

Photo by Simon Davis/ DFID, CC by SA 2.0

Soon she was being recognized in countries like South Africa, Britain, and Canada for her stance. She was nominated for the Youth Peace Prize. People in her home country were listening

On the Web

Tolerance.org has a pdf activity book about American Civil Rights for kids, probably suitable for 4th grade and up. You can get it here: http://www.tolerance.org/civil-rights-activity-book

Deep Thoughts

People often segregate themselves voluntarily. They live with, work with, hang out with, and worship with people who are most like themselves. Why do people do that? Is it good or bad?

Famous Folks

Liu Xiaobo was a Chinese civil rights activist who protested his country's abuses. He worked to end communist rule in China. He was imprisoned four times and won the Nobel Peace Prize while in jail the last time. He died in 2017 while still incarcerated. China has censored all mention of Liu, his peace prize, and his death.

These people, from Hong Kong, are protesting Liu's incarceration.

On the Web

Watch this 13 minute video "Nelson Mandela's Life Story" on YouTube: https://youtu.be/jgQ-BoXsxr8w. (This video discusses violence, it may not be suitable for your younger kids.)

Additional Layer

Think about the importance of education in the happiness and fulfillment of human beings. If you live in a developed western nation, you may be under the impression that the point of education is to get a good job. But it's so much more than that. Watch "25 Compelling Reasons Why Education Is Important" : https://youtu.be/h2LLPaIVNro.

Research more about the power of education and make a poster.

Additional Layer

Role play some situations your children might face where they would need courage. Here are some ideas:

Another child says you shouldn't be friends with someone.

An adult says you can't succeed.

To get a good job you have to leave your home town.

to her, and she was making a difference even at the top levels of government.

One day, when she was 14 as she rode a bus home from school, a Taliban gunman boarded the bus and demanded to know which girl was Malala. Then he shot her. But she didn't die. She was in critical care for months. As soon as she was well enough, she started speaking out again for educational rights for girls. In 2014 she was awarded the Nobel Peace Prize.

Education is one of the most important tools to help people be free and prosperous. Education also combats prejudice and fear, both sources of discrimination. Sometimes kids hate school and wish they didn't have to go, but what if you couldn't go?

At the end of this unit there is a schoolhouse printable. Print it on card stock. Cut it out on the outline. Color the front of the school. Inside the school you can draw pictures, write your thoughts about education rights, and find a quote from Malala that you like. Once you have finished coloring and writing, fold the schoolhouse and glue the tabs.

☺ ☺ ☺ EXPLORATION: Courage

The people who have made a positive change in the world have all had one thing in common: courage. They decided to speak out even when they knew they could be hurt or ridiculed for doing so. Most of them did pay the price for their stance. Martin Luther King Jr. was killed, Malala was shot, Nelson Mandela was jailed for years and years. They were sometimes afraid, but they spoke out anyway.

Courage can take many forms. You can have the courage to try something new, the courage to try again after you fail, the courage to stand up for someone who is being bullied, or the courage to be yourself even when you might get made fun of.

On a piece of paper write "Courage like _____." Fill in something that is a symbol of courage to you or write in the name of someone you admire. Then draw a picture of that thing or person in the center. Write down specific things you want to have the courage to do around it.

☺ EXPLORATION: Civil Rights Today

Search the news for a current event about civil rights. It could be in your country or somewhere else in the world. Determine which type of right is being offended or fought for. Is it a civil right, political right, or social right? Talk it over with a group, perhaps with your family over dinner or in a discussion with other youth. Do you agree that people should have the right that is being violated/fought for? Do you really think that right is being offended? Write a summary of what happened in the news story and your opinion about it.

Additional Layer

Some people say that human rights values are western values that are being pushed on countries of Asia and Africa in a form of modern imperialism. What do you think? Are the "rights" we've talked about universal or dependent on culture?

Famous Folks

Nabeel Rajab speaks out in Bahrain about human rights abuses. He is especially concerned about the plight of migrant workers in Persian Gulf countries.

Photo by Conor McCabe, CC by SA 2.0, Wikimedia

He has been arrested several times for speaking out on social media.

GEOGRAPHY: HOME STATE STUDY I

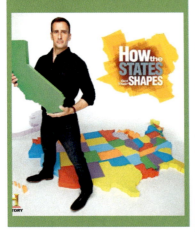
In this unit you're going to begin an in depth study of your home state. You will find activities that can apply to any state. During the unit you can make a map of your state, learn its history, and learn about state symbols and landmarks.

In Unit 4-19 you will learn about your state's constitution, government, natural resources, and economy.

☺ ☺ ☺ EXPLORATION: Big Map Project

You're going to make a detailed map of your state over the next two units, 4-18 and 4-19. It needs to be larger than a regular sheet of notebook paper so that you can really get in depth. There are a couple of ways to go about this. You can download any outline map of your state and have it printed poster size at a copy shop. We have all the printable state maps at Layers of Learning: www.layers-of-learning.com/geography/. Or you can have your kids draw a map freehand on a large sheet of paper. Both methods have their virtues.

During this unit, have your kids include the largest cities in your state as well as your home town, even if it is rather small. Also include your capital city, even if it isn't one of the larger cities. Youngest kids can add the top ten, middle grades the top twenty, and high schoolers the top thirty cities in terms of population.

Besides the cities, draw in mountains, rivers, lakes, and other natural features. Label them. Draw in the major highways and freeways and label them. Save your map. You'll add more to it in the next unit.

All map work should be done in ink and in the best possible handwriting. Don't color the map yet, we'll do that in the next unit.

☺ ☺ EXPLORATION: Your State's History
Create a timeline of your state's history. Your kids will have to research to find what happened in the history of your state. You can use images from the internet or draw pictures yourself to illustrate it. Encourage your kids to be creative with this project. It could just be a plain old wall timeline or you could make a movie, a roller box, a mobile, or use another method to make a fun timeline.

☺ ☺ ☺ EXPEDITION: Historical Site
Find out where a historical site is located near you in your state. Choose one you've never been to before if you can. Learn about the history of it and then go visit. While you're there take pictures or videos. Compile a tour of the site in a book, digital slide show, or video that you have narrated. Share it with your family or online.

☺ ☺ ☺ History Journal
Write a journal entry from a real or fictional person who experienced an event in your state. You can add some sketches to your journal entry as well.

If you like projects more than writing, then make a diorama of the event instead.

As you are driving from Montana into Idaho you cross some pretty tall mountains and go over 4th of July Pass, so called because that was the date John Mullen's road building crew took a break. The current freeway route is the same route of Mullen's initial road. Looking down from that point, all you see are mountains upon mountains in all directions. I try to imagine the initial job of building a road through that.

☺ ☺ ☺ EXPLORATION: I Love _____!
Interview as many people as possible about what they love about your state. Compile their comments in a book or video them

Additional Layer

Make a little book of weird facts about your state. Here's a weird story from our state of Idaho.

The town of Wallace, Idaho, population 759, is the center of the universe. No, really. It was declared by the mayor and they put it on a manhole cover in town.

Photo by Jan Kronsell, CC by SA 3.0

The idea came about when the EPA visited the little mining town and declared that the lead in the water was due to pollution, though they couldn't prove the lead wasn't naturally occurring. The EPA declared Wallace a Superfund site anyway. The mayor was furious and walked into the middle of town and declared Wallace to be the center of the universe.

This is based on the philosophy of probabilism. If you can't prove it isn't, then it is. Therefore, the city of Wallace decided that you can't prove Wallace isn't the center of the universe, so it must be.

Additional Layer

Every state in the U.S. was once home to native tribes or nations. Spend time learning about those who lived in your state.

Start by finding the local tribes on a map. http://www.native-languages.org/states.htm

Draw your own map of tribes in your state. Then choose one tribe to learn more about.

Make a notebook page:

- Homes
- Language
- Clothing
- Games & pastimes
- Travel
- Hunting, gathering, farming
- Modern places that are named in the tribe's language or after the tribe's leaders
- The history of the tribe
- News or information on current events in the tribe

talking. You can contact friends, neighbors, family members, the checker at the grocery store, random people walking down the street . . . anybody and everybody.

☺ ☻ EXPLORATION: State Symbols

Find out what your state symbols are and record them on a sheet for your notebook. You'll find a printable at the end of this unit on which to record your findings. In the boxes you can draw your state symbols or find pictures of them to print and paste in.

☺ ☻ ☻ EXPLORATION: State ABC Book

Make an alphabet book about your state. Look for things, people, places, or events from your state that start with each letter of the alphabet. Draw illustrations and write text for each page. We recommend using card stock or getting the book laminated and bound.

☺ ☻ ☻ EXPLORATION: State Travel Brochure

Create a travel brochure for your state. Choose a specific theme for your brochure. Do you want to highlight natural wonders, biggest attractions, best shopping, local gems, or places off the beaten path? You can use the printable brochure from Layers of Learning https://layers-of-learning.com/travel-brochure/ or craft your own (recommended for older kids).

☺ ☺ ☺ **EXPLORATION: Put Your State on the Web**
Build a website about your state. Include photos taken by you, articles written by you, maps drawn by you, and so on. Littler kids can do this project with the help of an adult.

We recommend using Google's Blogger. If you want to upgrade to your own domain name, it's the least expensive option and it's super easy to use.

☺ ☺ ☺ **EXPLORATION: Recipe Book**
Make a recipe book for your state. Include about ten different dishes. They should either be classic recipes that are made often in your state or they could have something to do with the natural resources or economy of your state. Idaho is definitely known for potatoes so I would probably put several potato recipes in my book. Rename your recipes to sound like your state. Make some of the dishes and have a feast.

☺ ☺ ☺ **EXPLORATION: Wildlife**
Look up information on the wildlife that lives in your state. Do you have any unique animals? Do you have any large predators or beautiful birds? Have you had any personal experiences with wildlife in your state? What animals do you see most often when you're driving or walking around?

On a sheet of paper, draw 6-8 animals that live in your state. Use how-to-draw guides from the internet. Label each animal with its name and put it in your notebook.

Additional Layer

Play State Scattergories using your home state.

https://layers-of-learning.com/layers-of-learning-printables/

On the Web

Crayola has printable state flag and symbols coloring pages, one for each state.

http://www.crayola.com/free-coloring-pages/history-and-social-studies/us-states-coloring-pages/

Writer's Notebook

Compile the information you've learned in this unit and make a lapbook about your home state. You can find a printable lapbook online or just make your own flaps and pockets that include your state's symbols, history, landmarks, food, and wildlife.

SCIENCE: INSTINCTS

On the Web

Khan Academy has a series of lessons on animal behavior here: https://www.khanacademy.org/science/biology/behavioral-biology/animal-behavior/a/intro-to-animal-behavior.

Have your high schooler read through and watch the videos.

Writer's Workshop

Animal behavior can be odd, as you know if you have any animals at your house. Once we came home to find a deer chasing our cat in the field next to the house. They went around and around in circles.

Another time we awakened in the night to find two raccoons dragging a plastic bin of dog food down our driveway. Due to earlier depredations we had lined the plastic bin with a wooden box and padlocked it shut. This didn't stop the raccoons even though they must have had to open the shop door to get the bin out in the first place.

Write down a funny or strange story you know about odd animal behavior.

Why do animals do what they do and look how they look? It's hard to know the answers to these questions for sure, but we can make some pretty good guesses.

Animals have some interesting behaviors that scientists describe as "instinct." Instinct means the animal does what it does out of biological impulses. A robin doesn't think about migrating south in the late fall, it just feels a strong impulse to do so without any understanding. This is instinct. We know that the robin migrates south because there isn't enough food for it in northern places where the plants die, the worms and insects sleep, and the ground is covered in snow. But does the robin know that? That's debatable.

People who study animals think that most of what an animal does is done by instinct, but some things are learned, passed on from generation to generation. A mother bear teaches her cubs to climb a tree if she gives the signal for danger. When the cubs grow up they will teach their own young the same thing. So some things animals do are done because of biological impulses, but some things are learned behaviors. Some things are a combination of instinct and learning.

The monarch butterfly is on the left and the viceroy butterfly on the right. Can you spot the differences?

Animals come in all sorts of colors from dull browns and grays to bright oranges, blues, and electric yellows. There are several theories about why particular animals are colored the way they are. It seems probable that deer are colored in dull browns in order to provide camouflage from their predators. It also seems likely that monarch butterflies are colored in bright orange to warn their potential predators that they taste bad. And, of course, the viceroy butterfly's coloring is almost certainly in mimicry of the monarch butterfly, to fool predators.

☺ ☻ ☻ EXPLORATION: Migration

Some animals, including birds, insects, fish, and mammals, migrate from place to place when conditions change. Deer migrate up to the mountains in spring and down to the valleys in winter. Whales migrate from arctic waters where they live in the summer to tropical waters where they live in the winter. Canadian geese migrate from the far north to the middle latitudes in winter. And monarch butterflies migrate from the north to the south in winter as well.

Many animals make the same migration journey year after year and perhaps learned the route from older members of their herd or flock. But the monarch is different. Monarch butterflies begin their southward migration from northern states and southern Canada in August. By October the monarch populations can be found in Mexico and southern California. They stay there over the winter and then return to the northern latitudes in the spring. But the lifespan of any one monarch butterfly is two months or less. So no single individual ever makes the entire trip. So how do they know where to go?

We don't exactly know. Scientists call this mysterious process instinct. But there are a few more specific theories. Some say the butterflies navigate by the position of the sun. Others say they can feel the earth's magnetic field, which acts like an internal compass. But the most mysterious part, how individuals find the massive butterfly colonies in the same locations year after year without any guides, is a complete mystery.

Watch this excellent film about the butterfly migration: http://youtu.be/lWjNZvWoAkE.

At the end of this unit you will find a map of the monarch's migration path to color.

☺ ☻ ☻ EXPLORATION: Hibernation

Winter is a tough time of year for animals. It gets cold, many plants die off, and deep snow covers the ground. There isn't much food or shelter. We saw above that monarch butterflies migrate south to avoid the cold weather. Other animals hibernate.

Hibernation is a state of deep sleep. The body temperature lowers, the heart rate slows way down, breathing slows, and metabolism drops steeply. This state conserves energy when there would not otherwise be enough for the animal to survive until spring.

To prepare for hibernation the animal eats lots and lots of food in the summer and fall to build up its energy reserves. Then it finds

Fabulous Fact

In Europe the painted lady butterfly makes a north and south migration between Northern Europe and Africa, similar to the monarch's flight.

On the Web

How do animals know where to migrate to, how do they navigate, and how do they know to go at all?

http://youtu.be/EbHS-kZySTBw

Additional Layer

Only pregnant female polar bears hibernate. Scientists are still working on figuring out why, but they think it may be related to the amount of nitrous oxide the bear's cells produce. Nitrous oxide affects metabolism.

Famous Folks

Technically, only endotherms, warm-blooded animals, hibernate. The definition of hibernation includes a drop in body temperature and metabolism. Reptiles and amphibians are ectotherms, their body temperature can't be dropped below a "norm." Instead they do something called brumation. They find a protected and sufficiently warm hole to climb into and sleep the winter away, waking only to drink water once in a while. The only real difference is in the metabolic processes the body goes through.

Fabulous Fact

Some animals sleep a lot in the winter but wake up from time to time. Their heart rate slows and their breathing slows, but they are not in deep hibernation. If you poke them they will wake up mad. Some scientists say this isn't really hibernation at all, but only torpor, while others say, it is hibernation. The debates about metabolic rates are tedious. For the purposes of this unit, any animal that sleeps away most of the winter in a den or hole is hibernating.

a safe hole or den to curl up in and falls asleep. Animals can sleep for weeks or months depending on the species and the weather conditions. The animal wakes up as the temperatures outside begin to rise again.

Use the "How Hibernation Works" printable from the end of this unit. Describe what happens in the fall to prepare the animals for hibernation, and then describe what happens to the animal while it is in hibernation. You can adapt this assignment to the level of your children. For younger kids, find a picture book that talks about hibernation. Then have your child fill out the sheet.

Older kids, 7th grade and up, can read "How Hibernation Works" from HowStuffWorks.com (http://animals.howstuffworks.com/animal-facts/hibernation.htm), and use that information to fill out the sheet. You can color the bears and make a flap to cover the hibernating bear with "snow" if you like.

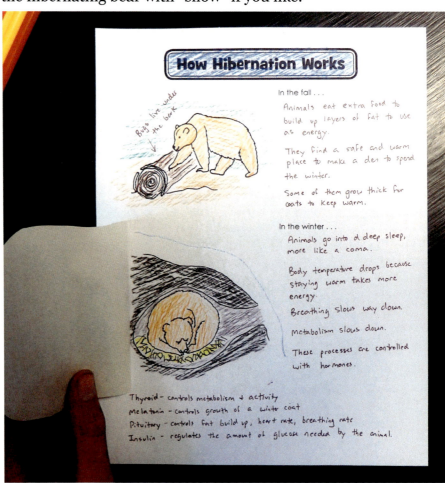

☻ ☻ ☻ **EXPLORATION: Hibernacula**
The place an animal hibernates in, its den, is called a hibernacula. Hibernacula is Latin for "winter tent quarters." Lady beetles

congregate together in large groups in the crevices of rocks. Frogs burrow into mud below the frost line. The alpine newt hibernates in dead logs. The European viper will slither into any rock pile, a rodent tunnel, cave, crevice, or ant mound it can find. Black bears excavate a den in the side of a hill or sometimes find a dry cave. Marmots dig deep burrows into the sides of hills. Night crawlers burrow down 6 feet, line their burrow with mucus to stay moist, and stay there all winter. Hedgehogs drag thick layers of dead leaves, twigs, and grass into a protected space like under a shed, under the roots of a tree, or in an old rabbit den.

Choose a type of animal hibernacula from the descriptions above or another you have read about. Make a model of it by cutting off one side of a small box and decorating the inside of the box to look like the den. You can also use stiff paper and make the paper into a box. Put the animal inside the den.

Additional Layer

Some animals' coloring is just incidental. Worms are pinkish because their blood is red and it shows through their white skin. Since worms spend most of their time under the ground they don't need any special coloring.

Fabulous Facts

This is a yellow banded poison dart frog, one of a group of frogs of various species all found in Central and South America.

Some species of dart frog are very poisonous. They excrete poison through their skin, which, when touched, can lead to heart failure even in an adult human or large animal. Dart frogs are always brightly colored to warn predators.

☺ ☻ **EXPLORATION: Where Do Animals Go In Winter?** Some animals just stay put all winter. They don't migrate and they don't hibernate. Rabbits, deer, squirrels, foxes, wolves, and fish stay active all winter. Some of them change their behaviors to protect from the cold. For example, squirrels cache large amounts of food in their dens and eat off their stores all winter. Deer don't migrate south, but they do come down out of the mountains into the valleys where the snow isn't quite so deep so they can dig through to find last year's grass. Owls switch from hunting only at night to hunting nearly all the time. They listen for the tell-

Famous Folks

Some animals have bioluminescence. They actually glow. Some, like the firefly, use this to attract other fireflies. Others, like the angler fish, use their glow to attract prey. And still others may use the glow to warn off predators.

Fabulous Fact

This is an animal called the orange elephant ear sponge. It is bright orange to warn would-be predators that it tastes awful.

Insects aren't the only ones who use warnings.

tale sounds of rodents in their tunnels under the snow and then dive right into the snow, snatching the rodent. They also hunt for things they wouldn't bother with in summer months, like small birds. For all of these animals, winter is always a leaner time of year and more of them die in the winter than at other times.

Draw two circles of the same size on two separate pieces of card stock. The circles should take up most of the paper. Divide one circle into three equal parts. Write "migrate," "hibernate," and "stay put" in each of the three sections. Draw an example of an animal that exhibits that behavior in each section, then write a short description of what that behavior means for the animal in winter. On the other circle cut away 1/3 to make a window. Write "Animals in Winter" on it. Attach the two circles together with a brad so that your window can move from section to section.

☺ ☻ ☻ EXPLORATION: Animal Colors

At the end of this unit you will find printable animal cards. Each card has a picture of an animal and its name. Sort the animals into one of six categories. You'll need six sheets of paper. Write a type of animal coloring at the top of each sheet. Then paste the animal cards that fit that coloring category on that page. For example, if you have a picture of a skunk, you'll put the skunk on the "Warning" page, because the bold white stripe down a skunk's back warns other animals (except for some reason the family dog) that tangling with the skunk will be a bad idea.

Here are the page titles and the definitions:

- <u>Camouflage</u> – An animal that blends into or is hidden in its environment by its coloring or even body shape.
- <u>Signaling</u> – An animal that sends messages to other animals with its body coloring, like the cleaner wrasse which turns bright blue to let other fish know it is available for services or the bright plumage on the male peacock that lets the peahen know he's interested in her.
- <u>Warning</u> – The coloring of dangerous animals is often bright or very noticeable to let potential predators know they should back off.
- <u>Mimicry</u> – Sometimes a harmless animal's body coloring is a copy, or close copy, of a dangerous animal's, to fool predators.
- <u>Distraction</u> – Animals that have coloring that confuses the eye, like a zebra in a herd, or that startles a predator, like the big "eye" spots on the wings of some moths, can distract or confuse a predator.
- <u>Physical Protection</u> – Some animals are colored to prevent sunburn or can change the color of their skin to either absorb extra heat or reflect it to maintain their body temperature.

If you're not sure which category an animal fits into, look up more information about the animal. It's possible an animal could fit in more than one category. Scientists just arrange animals the way they like and the way you like is not less valid as long as you have a good reason. You may want to find more pictures of animals to add your pages.

☺ ☺ EXPLORATION: Danger!

Some animals are brightly colored and their coloring is a warning to other animals that would eat them. For example, the cinnabar moth eats ragwort, a poisonous plant, which also makes the moth poisonous. The cinnabar moth has bright red markings on its black wings. The bright red markings warn birds, lizards, snakes and other predators that eating this moth would be a bad idea.

Choose one of these poisonous butterflies or moths, learn more about it, and create a craft that shows off its warning markings.

- Monarch butterfly
- Cinnabar moth
- Giant African swallowtail
- Pipevine swallowtail
- Tiger moth

First, paint your hands in the colors of the butterfly you chose. Then press your hands on to a sheet of white paper. Paint the butterfly's body. After the paint has dried you can add on feelers,

---

Additional Layer

Human beings have different coloration, or amounts of melanin in their skin and hair. Traditionally, before the modern mass migrations, people who lived closer to the equator had dark skin and hair while those who live in the upper latitudes had lighter skin and hair.

Why is skin color distributed the way it is?

Additional Layer

The great tit, a bird from Europe, Asia, and northern Africa, instinctively avoids the bright danger signals of insects. Each individual bird does not have to have had experience to avoid the bad tasting prey. How does that work? It's a mystery.

Photo by Bengt Nyman, CC license, Wikimedia

legs, and the name of your butterfly.

Additional Layer

Some animals change color depending on their environment. The arctic fox is white in winter and brown in summer.

The change in amount of daylight creates a hormonal change in the fox that changes the color of its hair.

Cuttlefish can constrict muscles which squeeze the pigment in their cells and cause color changes depending on their surroundings.

Chameleons change colors depending on their mood.

Nudibranches feed on coral and their bodies take on the color of whatever kind of coral they are feeding on at the moment, creating perfect camouflage.

Learn more about these animals.

☺ **EXPLORATION: Hide and Seek**

Camouflage helps animals hide. They may want to hide from predators or they may want to sneak up on prey.

A dolphin has dark gray skin on top of its body, fading to white on its underside. So if you look down in the water at a dolphin it is hard to see against the dark background of the deep water. If you are under the water and looking up, it is hard to see the dolphin against the bright light of the surface.

An arctic hare's fur turns white in the winter when the world is covered in snow. In the summer its fur is brown. How does changing the color of its fur help it hide from predators?

A praying mantis is waiting for an insect to come along, maybe an ant or a cricket. It will hide in the tree still as can be and then suddenly strike. It's also watching out for birds, bats, frogs, and snakes. Its coloring and body shape help it both hunt and hide.

Go to your closet and find some clothes that will help you camouflage in your backyard or a nearby park. Usually browns and dull greens are best. Black works well and so does gray. Put on the clothes and then play a game of hide and seek. Do you think it would be harder to hide in your yard if you were wearing bright clothes? Try it.

☺ ☺ ☺ EXPERIMENT: Does Camouflage Work?

Get a sheet of newspaper and lay it out on the floor. Choose a page that has only text with no pictures. Then prepare 8-10 rectangles of paper, all the same size. About half of these should be cut out of newspaper (remember - no pictures!). The others can be white or brightly colored. Lay all the rectangles on the paper.

Then cover a friend's eyes and have them walk into the room. Let them look at the paper for one second, then cover their eyes again. How many rectangles did the friend see?

Take turns having different people try with different numbers of rectangles. Record the results. Was the camouflage effective?

Animals in the wild often have only a moment to see the predator or the prey before they must act, just like you had only a moment to see the rectangles of paper.

☺ ☺ ☺ EXPERIMENT: The Stimulus of Color

Animals respond to stimuli in their environment. A stimulus is something that arouses activity. Heat, cold, a loud noise, the presence of food, or the sight of a predator might evoke a response in an animal. Sometimes when we speak of animals we talk about them as though they are making decisions about how to behave. We might say that the moth flares its wings to scare away predators. The truth is, we have no idea whether the moth knows it is flaring its wings to scare away predators or if this is an involuntary response to a stimulus, in other words, an instinct.

One stimulus an animal may respond to is color. Get four bird feeders and paint each one completely in a different color. Try some bright and some darker colors.

Set them out with the same amount of food in locations near one another in your yard. Keep an eye on the bird feeder for a few days. Do you notice a pattern? Does one bird feeder get visited more often than another? Try moving the bird feeders, swapping places with one another. Then watch again. Did one bird feeder

Additional Layer

Foraging is how animals find food. Some foraging behaviors are instinctual and some are learned. It can be difficult sometimes to determine which are which. Do wolves hunt in packs because they have learned this is the best way to obtain prey, or do they do it because of a social instinct?

Read up on different animals and their ways of gathering food. Do you see any patterns of behaviors?

Fabulous Fact

When we speak of animals "learning" we mean that a single individual has learned a behavior in response to stimulus. A species as a whole may be able to learn (or not, there's not enough data yet) and pass on that learning. But when behaviors are passed on genetically we call this instinct.

Fabulous Fact

Humans are so good at learning and reasoning that it may appear that we have no instincts. But reflexes and some of the things babies do, like rooting and grasping a finger tightly, are instinctual.

On the Web

"Response to External Environments" from Bozeman Science is a video that talks about how animals respond to their environment. It includes hibernation, migration, and physiological responses. https://youtu.be/BUlBwe8miTQ

Additional Layer

Intuition is knowing something without being able to explain how you know. It is akin to instinct. Some people can gather cues, or behaviors of others, and synthesize them into a set of data that leads to a conclusion. They do this so instinctively that they don't realize they are even collecting the information. Intuitive people usually have high emotional intelligence.

Additional Layer

Dogs instinctively shake after getting wet. This drying process is more complex than you might think. Read "Science Looks at Why and How Wet Dogs Shake" from Psychology Today: https://www.psychologytoday.com/blog/canine-corner/201209/science-looks-why-and-how-wet-dogs-shake.

get visited more often than another? Was it the same one as before?

You can try this experiment with hummingbird feeders instead if you like. Buy 2 hummingbird feeders and paint them one a dull color, leaving one red. Fill them with identical nectar.

☺ ☺ ☺ **EXPERIMENT: The Stimulus of Light**
Animals respond to light in different ways. Design an experiment to test how light affects an animal. Choose either a daphnia culture (Home Science Tools or a pet store) or a goldfish. You will also need a small tank of water and food for your animals.

You can test for responses to light due to

• Color
• Position

Remember to have a control and make your test conditions the same except for one variable. Record your findings and include photographs or illustrations.

☺ ☺ ☺ **EXPERIMENT: The Stimulus of Smell**
Animals respond to smell stimulus too. Design an experiment to figure out what attracts or repels mosquitoes. Mosquitoes mostly eat the nectar of flowers. Only the females suck blood just before laying eggs because they need the protein for their egg formation. We do know that mosquitoes are attracted by carbon dioxide, which you breath. You can produce carbon dioxide by growing

yeast in warm water with some sugar.

Rumor has it that mosquitoes are repelled by cinnamon, citronella oil, peppermint, basil oil, and garlic.

To do a proper test you need to find something that attracts the mosquitoes first. Then add some repellent on top of your attractant. For example you might sprinkle cinnamon on bananas.

You also need a way to trap the mosquitoes. Vegetable oil and water with some dish soap to break the surface tension are both good traps, so use them with your attractant/repellent.

☺ ☺ ☺ **EXPERIMENT: The Stimulus of Temperature**
For this experiment you will need crickets, a home for your crickets to live in (an aquarium or plastic habitat box with a vented lid), food (oats, bran, fish food, vegetables), and a sponge soaked in water so your crickets can drink.

Design an experiment to test how different temperatures affect the cricket's "singing." Use heat packs or ice packs to gently raise and lower the temperature. Use a thermometer to measure the temperature. Record your data.

Additional Layer

Imprinting is learning that must take place at a certain phase of development. An example is baby geese that learn who their mother is and then follow her around.

Photo by Superbass / CC-BY-SA-3.0, Wikimedia.

In the photo above these geese have imprinted on the pilot of the ultralight. The movie "Fly Away Home" tells the story of geese that imprinted on a human.

Attachment disorder is a sad case of a human child failing to learn to become attached to human beings because during a critical period in the child's life (birth to age 2) he or she was isolated or abused. People who have never imprinted on others during this stage lose the ability to form attachments or care about other human beings.

Learn about imprinting of animals and humans and how critical parental care of young is to normal biological development. You may also be interested in researching "attachment styles."

THE ARTS: THEATER & FILM

Famous Folks

Florence Lawrence is known as the first movie star. Her first stage show was at just 3 years old. She was hired by Thomas Edison's movie studios to act, and then began filming movies for their studios. She was the very first person ever to be named in a movie and starred in almost 250 silent films in the early 1900s.

Theater and film have become important pieces of the art world in our modern times. How many shows would you predict you've seen in the past year? Do you have any favorite actors or actresses? Between stages, theaters, and the televisions and computers within our own homes, shows are a very pervasive part of our everyday lives. This unit will include historical and modern information about theater and film, along with some practical explorations for those who enjoy drama and want to have some experiences in the world of acting or working behind the scenes of a show.

Theater is the art of telling stories by acting them out live. Movies are also acted out, but are recorded on film, edited, and often enhanced using sound effects, camera tricks, and computer animations and graphics. How do you think shows (both plays and movies) tell stories differently than reading a book or listening to a story?

☺ ☺ ☺ **EXPLORATION: Plays and Movies**
Make a Venn diagram together while you discuss some similarities and differences between plays and movies. How are they alike? Can you think of any important differences between live plays and movies we see in theaters?

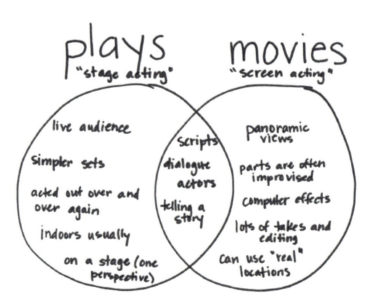

☺ ☺ ☺ **EXPLORATION: History of the Theater**
People have been putting on plays for entertainment since ancient times. Watch this video, History of Theater, to learn about how this art has evolved over time: http://bit.ly/2vtS5yW.

Use the History of the Theater printable with the comedy and tragedy masks to make a learning web from the information in the video. Write down categories she discusses in the circles, then draw lines from each circle with things you learned about that topic. Here is the beginning of a web that shows the categories and some details from the section on the Greeks.

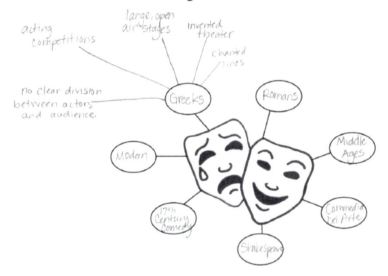

History of the Theater

😊 😊 😊 **EXPLORATION: History of Film**

Watch "Movies are Magic: Crash Course Film History #1" and "The First Movie Camera: Crash Course History #2" from YouTube. You'll learn about the happy accident that led to the beginning of film and also have a great review of the photography section of Unit 4-16.

https://youtu.be/vsnB4iBb78o

https://youtu.be/pKSmcmueTbA

Make your own stop motion picture using toys. Set up a scene using legos or small toy figurines. If possible, put your camera on a tripod so it won't move. If you don't have a tripod, you can set your camera on a small stool or a stack of books. Try to keep it as still as possible.

Once you have your first picture, move the toy figure just a bit. Take another photo. Keep making small changes and taking pictures, creating a storyline with the movements. You should take around 200 pictures. Put them all on your computer, keeping them in their original order, and then use basic movie-maker software to show the pictures in order. Set the slide time to last

Fabulous Fact

Hollywood became the center of the film industry after Thomas Edison's company, who held movie making patents, began suing people to stop their productions. Filmmakers headed out west where the patents weren't being enforced.

Additional Layer

Acting students play a game called Mirror Acting. You can play it too. Get a partner and choose one person to be the leader and the other to be the mirror reflection. The leader moves very slowly while the mirror reflects each action, trying to duplicate every movement, action, and facial expression. The goal is to be so in sync that spectators cannot tell who the leader is and who the mirror is.

Teaching Tips

Here's a simple stop motion movie made by a kid to help you get an idea for how it's done. It's called "How To Make a Stop Motion Animation With Toys - Home Activity with Kids - DIY" by PlaneTree Family.

https://youtu.be/sD-BuO995zW8

Additional Layer

Learn a monologue. Mono means one, so a monologue is a speech by one person. Rather than a conversation, which goes back and forth between two or more people, a monologue just has one person talking. Often they are thinking through things aloud. This website has a list of monologues for girls and another for boys. Many are quite long and will take a lot of work to memorize. Memory work is a great and worthwhile skill though. https://www.theatrefolk. com/free-resources

The website also has lots of lessons about writing plays, acting, and performing monologues.

Writer's Workshop

Write your own play or movie script. Remember that although you can include stage directions, most of the action needs to come from dialogue.

Younger kids can make their own version of an already familiar tale. You can use a picture book that has a story they know well or a fairy tale, and then have them help create the words the characters will say.

only .125 seconds each. That means that every 8 pictures you take will play per second. So if you have 200 pictures, your movie will be 25 seconds long. When you play it back it will look like your characters are moving and you can see the link between photography and motion pictures.

☺ ☺ ☺ EXPLORATION: Expressions and Movements

In a portrait, the painter must include emotion in the face and body of the person. In plays and movies, it is up to the actors to show those emotions. As viewers, we notice tiny things that give us clues about what people are thinking and feeling. Think about what your face might look like if you're lonely. Now compare that with how it might look as you walk into your own surprise party, just at the moment the guests jump out and yell, "Surprise!" Actors try to mimic the facial expressions and body movements that people have in real situations, even though they aren't going through them in real life. (It's pretty hard to actually BE surprised if you've memorized the script and know what's coming!)

Play a game to practice showing emotions. Write these emotions on index cards or small slips of paper: happy, sad, angry, surprised, embarrassed, hopeful, annoyed, nervous, shy, curious, excited, grateful, peaceful, frustrated, proud, fascinated, in love. It might be helpful to get online and look at pictures of people displaying those emotions and point out the things you see.

Take turns drawing one out and acting out that emotion. Think about both your facial expressions and what your whole body can do to show an emotion. Everyone watching must try to guess the emotion. Take turns acting and guessing.

This is clearly a sad girl. Her face is turned down. She is frowning. Her eyes are lowered and her eyebrows are furrowed. Can you make a sad face?

☺ ☺ ☺ EXPLORATION: What Makes a Great Actor?

Actors often train for many, many years to become effective. It is their job to become their character so the audience feels connected with them and with the story.

Brainstorm together some things that make a good actor. You might include things like a loud, clear voice, a team player, someone who is expressive, a focused person who doesn't goof off, someone who likes being in front of people or the center of attention, a person who is really good at following directions.

Make a series of paper bag puppets who are all different characters. Create a two year old little boy, a cowgirl, a businessman, a teenager, an angry person, a bubbly lady, and an athlete. You can choose to make more character puppets if you would like to.

Give each kid a puppet to be their "actor" or "actress." Give them a simple line to have their puppet say. Here are a few ideas:

"I want some ice cream now."

"How do you get out of here?"

"My favorite foods are all yellow - bananas, lemons, and cheese."

If it is the two year old boy puppet, he might be begging and whining while he delivers the line: "I want some ice cream now." Now have the bubbly lady puppet deliver the same line. Practice the various lines in the voices of the different puppets.

☺ ☺ ☺ EXPLORATION: Create A Set

Scenery is the backdrop for a play. Scenery isn't always completely realistic, but it helps the audience to see a glimpse of the setting of the story. Even though they are sitting in an indoor theater, simple scenery can transport the audience to an outdoor picnic on the beach, a racetrack, a scary castle, a deep forest, or anywhere.

Use a large piece of canvas or another plain fabric to create your own scenery for your set. Canvas is the best because it is very sturdy, but a large, white flat bed sheet is a great and inexpensive alternative. You'll need to think of a scene and what elements belong in that scene. Close your eyes and picture a scene. What do you imagine it to look like? Notice all of the small details. Make a quick sketch on a sheet of paper, then begin using pencil to draw your set design right on your fabric backdrop. Sketch your entire background on the sheet before beginning to paint.

The painting of play sets is usually done in 3 layers.

1. Background Layer - You'll begin by painting the background layer. Use an equal ratio of your paint color, white paint, and water. The water will help your paint to quickly and lightly

Famous Folks

Charlie Chaplin was an iconic early film star. He was known for his slapstick style. He not only acted, but also wrote, produced, and directed a lot of his movies. He even wrote the music that ran under the film.

Famous Folks

Choose a famous person from the movie industry to research. If possible, read their biography and write a one page bio sheet about him or her.

Walt Disney

Steven Spielberg

Marlon Brando

Alfred Hitchcock

John Williams

Gene Kelly

Katharine Hepburn

Marilyn Monroe

Judy Garland

George Lucas

Additional Layer

Freeze and Justify is a classic improv game. Two people begin to improvise a scene. At any moment an audience member can shout, "Freeze!" The two must freeze in place, then the audience member who froze them steps up, taps one on the shoulder, and takes the place of the frozen actor. He or she must resume the acting, but based on a new scene or storyline that uses the body positions they are already in. The topic of the new scene must be communicated through acting.

spread and cover more of your scene. When you are done with your background layer, your whole sheet will be covered with paint.

2. Objects Layer - You'll add objects into your scene to make it more interesting. You want more vivid colors for this layer. That means you should use the paint colors straight, without adding white paint or water.

3. Highlight, Detail, and Define Layer - For this layer you will add

details and make your objects stand out more. If you drew a tree on your objects layer, you might add apples to it, for example. You can also just simply highlight objects by mixing the color of paint you used on your object with a little white, creating a new tint of that color that you apply to certain areas to give dimension to the object. You can also add shadows by adding a touch of darker paint for the shaded areas. Finally, you will use black to trace around certain objects so they stand out.

Remember, this isn't meant to be a perfectly realistic scene. It's meant to represent a location, and you want the people at the very back of the theater to be able to understand your setting at a quick glance, so rather than tiny details, focus on the overall setting and a few important objects.

Once your scene is dry, you can sew (or just fold over and glue) a pocket seam across the top. Attach a piece of PVC pipe or an inexpensive curtain rod and hang it on a wall. There are removable adhesive hooks that are strong enough to hold it up on your wall. They can then be removed when you're done play acting with your scene.

☺ ☺ ☺ EXPLORATION: Areas of the Stage

Memorize the areas of a stage and a few other important parts of a theater. Use sidewalk chalk to practice drawing and labeling them outside in a large open area. Alternatively, write each location on a piece of paper and practice laying out the papers on the

Teaching Tip

The toughest part about the Create A Set Exploration is the size. It can be tough to make things on such a large scale. Step back and look at your work often to make sure you have the proper scale. If you need to, draw a grid on your sketch and another one on your canvas. It can help you to keep things proportional even on such a large backdrop.

Fabulous Fact

Animated films have sets and characters that are drawn and manipulated using computer animation. In *Monsters, Inc.*, Sully had 2,320,413 hairs that were all individually animated.

On The Web

Watch this short film called Pixar's Zoetrope by AnimationIL to learn all about how animation works and find out what a Zoetrope is. https://youtu.be/5khDGKGvo88

Toy Story Zoetrope. Photo by Josh Hallet and shared under CC 2.0 license.

Expedition

Once you've learned the parts of a stage, make arrangements to go visit a theater when there isn't a show going on. You will be able to walk around the backstage areas, see the control booth, examine the catwalk, and walk around the stage, identifying the different areas. Play a game where you call out a stage direction and the kids must all go to that spot on the stage to show what they've memorized.

Additional Layer

Learn the jobs in the show with a game. Take on the role of one job at a time and describe what you're doing. "I'm sewing a skirt for a poodle in the show. What am I?" (A costume designer)

On The Web

You can go visit this site to see "25 Abandoned Movie Sets You Can Still Visit." Even if you can't actually go visit, it's cool to see the pictures and read a bit about them. Warning: this is an entertainment site with changing ads; please preview or view with your kids. http://list25.com/25-abandoned-movie-sets-you-can-still-visit/

ground in the right spot. Play a game where the space is called out and the kids must go to that area of the stage.

The stage is divided into two areas - the playing space, or the area of the stage that is visible to the audience, and the backstage, which is a place the actors go when they are not in the scene. They can change costumes, touch up stage make-up, and prepare to enter the playing area when it is their turn. The backstage area also allows them to travel between stage left and stage right without being seen.

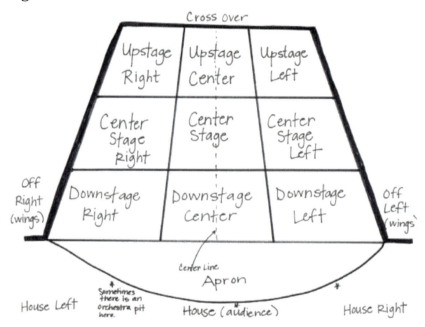

Besides the locations shown, there is often a catwalk hanging above the stage which holds lighting, microphones, and other special equipment. At the rear of the theater, behind the house, there is typically a control booth with a board that manipulates the lighting and sound. Sometimes there are also balconies or box seats where additional audience members can sit.

☺ ☺ EXPLORATION: Jobs in the Show

Make a booklet that tells about some basic jobs of people who work in the theater and film industry. Each page will have one job description, along with an illustration of a person or group of people doing that job.

- Producer: funds the show and hires a director
- Publicity team: advertises and promotes the play
- Director: leads the rehearsals and interprets the script, giving directions for how scenes should look and sound and what actors should do. Also works with an assistant director.
- Stage Manager/Assistant Stage Manager: Run the stage from

the backstage area, including lights, sound, props, and scenery. Work with a backstage crew to move props and scenery in and out during the show or filming.

- Actors: Memorize and then recite lines; they try to become their characters for the show, doing what the characters would do.
- Set Designer: Creates sets and scenery. Works with a construction and paint crew to actually build sets or secure needed locations or supplies for the sets. There is also a prop designer and team who works with the set designer.
- Sound Designer: Coordinates all sounds, from microphones to music and sound effects. Works with a sound crew.
- Lighting Designer: Plans and executes the lighting for each scene, has many kinds of colorful lights to help create different moods. Works with a lighting crew.
- Costume Designer: Plans and creates or finds costumes for all of the characters. Works with a crew. Make-up designers are also part of the creative team that help bring characters to life.
- Special Effects/Stunts Team: They plan and execute difficult or dangerous parts of the show that require their expertise.

The costumes and set can be quite over the top in the theater. This is from a play called "Hansel and Gretel," based on the famous fairy tale.

☺ ☺ ☺ EXPLORATION: Working on a Movie Set

Movie sets are very different from the scenery and stage of a play. Sometimes they are filmed on sound stages, which are like giant warehouses where realistic sets are built. Often they are filmed in

Fabulous Fact

Even though they aren't modern, William Shakespeare's plays are still the most famous of all time. *Hamlet* and *Romeo and Juliet* are two of the most famous. Besides Shakespeare, Arthur Miller's *Death of Salesman* and Oscar Wilde's *The Importance of Being Earnest* top the most famous plays list.

Additional Layer

It's hard to make a list of the most popular movies of all time, because art is very subjective. Here are some important shows based on popularity and number of tickets sold. How many have you seen?

Star Wars

The Sound of Music

E.T.

Titanic

Jaws

Snow White and the Seven Dwarfs

Gone With the Wind

Harry Potter

Frozen

The Ten Commandments

The Wizard of Oz

The Lion King

Mary Poppins

Raiders of the Lost Ark

On The Web

Watch this cool behind the scenes look at some real life action movie stunts and how they were done. The clip is called "2 Fast 2 Furious - Stunts and Special Effects" by WAusJackBauer.

https://youtu.be/NNcl-j8Ek8uo

Teaching Tip

Choose a script from scripts.com that you own the movie for. First, read the scene aloud, then watch that same scene from the movie as it plays out on the screen. The script is important, but the actors, effects, sound, and other factors all bring the script to life.

Writer's Workshop

Use the outline on this page as you write your own script. It could be a short scene all of the way up to an entire movie. Make sure to follow the outline, have a clear nemesis and hero, and include dialogue, along with descriptions of what is happening in each scene.

real locations around the world though. If a jungle scene will be filmed, they go to the jungle. If a busy street is needed, the cast and crew head to the city. If the movie demands a desert scene, they travel to a desert to film.

There are a lot of people who all work together to make sure all the parts of a movie come together - the acting, the sets, the cameras, the lighting, the effects, and all of the logistics that go into a film. The director, producer, actors, special effects crew, lighting specialists, art department, and many more people all do their specific jobs. Watch "The Making of Jurassic Park" by The Jurassic Collection on YouTube to get a peek at what goes into a movie. Please be aware that it shows scenes from the movie, so if this dinosaur show is too scary or mature for your kids, this video will be too. It also lasts nearly an hour. It's a pretty neat peek at how they made this thrilling film and brought dinosaurs to life on screen though. https://youtu.be/TUVAirMVru0

😊 😊 😊 EXPLORATION: Special Effects and Stunts
Universal Studios in Hollywood, California puts on a show that demonstrates how a lot of special effects are done in movies. You can watch their show online. https://youtu.be/k0d1wwzbM4E

😊 😊 EXPLORATION: Writing A Script
A big part of any play or movie is the script. The script is the written story. It lists the lines of each character, stage directions, and descriptions of the basic plot as it is unfolding.

Scripts have three parts. Here is an outline of a basic script.
I. The Overview
    A. One-Liner (a one line description of what the play or movie is about)
    B. The Background (A bit about how the characters got involved in the story)
    C. The Premise (a 1-3 paragraph more detailed overview of the storyline)
    D. The Nemesis (a description of the villains who will create problems)
    E. The Hero (a description of the hero)
II. The Beat Sheet
    A. A Breakdown of Each Scene
    B. Each section of the breakdown includes a numbered list of the bits of action that will happen in the scene.
III. The Script
    A. Stage and camera directions
    B. Scene descriptions

C. Lines

Scripts.com is a website repository of movie scripts. They generally only share the third section of the above outline - the actual script, not the overview nor the beat sheet. You can look at scripts from familiar shows to see what the movies looked like when they were just on paper. There are many to choose from. "Inside Out" would be a great script for kids to examine, and it's included on the site. Assign several people to be characters. A parent can read the stage directions. Try reading a scene from the script aloud. How does it compare with watching the same scene in the movie?

☺ ☺ ☺ **EXPLORATION: Act It Out**

Go visit www.dramanote-book.com/plays-for-kids and select a play. They describe the number of parts and pages right in the description. Assign parts and learn the lines. Work together to be the creative team. Put together a simple play, practice, and perform it.

☺ ☺ ☺ **EXPEDITION: Going To The Show**

To end this unit, go see a show. You might see a live play on a real stage, or go to the movie theater and watch a movie. During the car ride, recall together the things you've learned and practiced during this unit.

Fabulous Fact

People spend a lot of money making movies. It's considered normal for major films to cost over a hundred million dollars to create. Pirates of the Caribbean: On Stranger Tides had a budget of 378.5 trillion dollars. That's expensive art.

Writer's Workshop

Think of your very favorite character from a play or movie. What makes that one your favorite? Do you connect with the character somehow? Is it the hero, the villain, or someone extra from the story? Write about what you think makes a great character and what you think makes people connect with characters.

Coming up next . . .

Unit 4-19

Technology
Home State Study II
Habitats
Architecture

My ideas for this unit:

Title: _____ **Topic:** _____

_____
_____
_____
_____
_____
_____
_____
_____
_____
_____
_____

Title: _____ **Topic:** _____

_____
_____
_____
_____
_____
_____
_____
_____
_____
_____
_____
_____

Title: _____ **Topic:** _____

_____
_____
_____
_____
_____
_____
_____
_____
_____
_____
_____

Title: _____ **Topic:** _____

_____
_____
_____
_____
_____
_____
_____
_____
_____
_____

Title: _____ **Topic:** _____

_____
_____
_____
_____
_____
_____
_____
_____
_____
_____
_____

Title: _____ **Topic:** _____

_____
_____
_____
_____
_____
_____
_____
_____
_____
_____

Civil Rights

These men are at a civil rights rally in the United States in the 1960s. Black men and women were not being treated fairly by the governments they lived under. They experienced systematic discrimination that prevented them from getting an education, running a business, or getting a job. Sometimes they were unfairly accused of crimes and then tried by stacked juries that found them guilty no matter the truth. In some places white people could attack or even kill black people, and the law would do nothing. The Civil Rights Movement in the United States was successful in meeting the goal of removing discrimination from government, but prejudice is still in the hearts of many people.

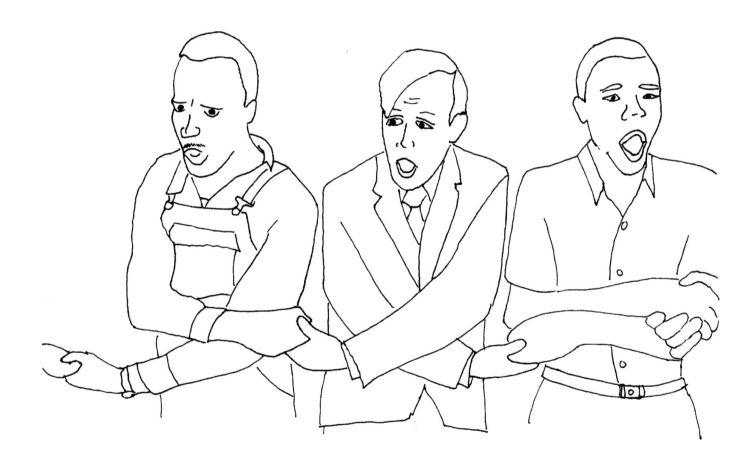

Civil Rights Timeline

1789	**1793**	**1848**	**1866**
The U.S. Bill of Rights is adopted	France writes the Declaration of the Rights of Man and of the Citizen	Seneca Falls, New York Conference on Women's Rights	Civil Rights Bill to protect newly freed blacks in the U.S. passed

1893	**1900-1920s**	**1920s**	**Dec 1948**
New Zealand is the first country to give women the right to vote in national elections	Women achieve the right to vote in many western nations (U.S. 1920, U.K. 1918)	Laws are passed to protect the civil rights of Catholics in England	UN drafts the Universal Declaration of Human Rights

1950s-1960s	**1981**	**1994**	
Civil rights movement to give blacks equality in America	Mauritania outlaws slavery, the last country to do so	Blacks are allowed to vote in South African elections and apartheid is finally over	

Civil Rights	Political Rights	Social Rights
The right to bear arms	The right to vote	The right to not be discriminated against in a place of business
The right to free speech	The right to run for elected office	The right to an education
The right to worship freely	The right to serve on a jury	The right to work
The right to a fair trial		The right to healthcare
The right to privacy		The right to not be discriminated against in housing
The right to freely trade		The right to rest and leisure

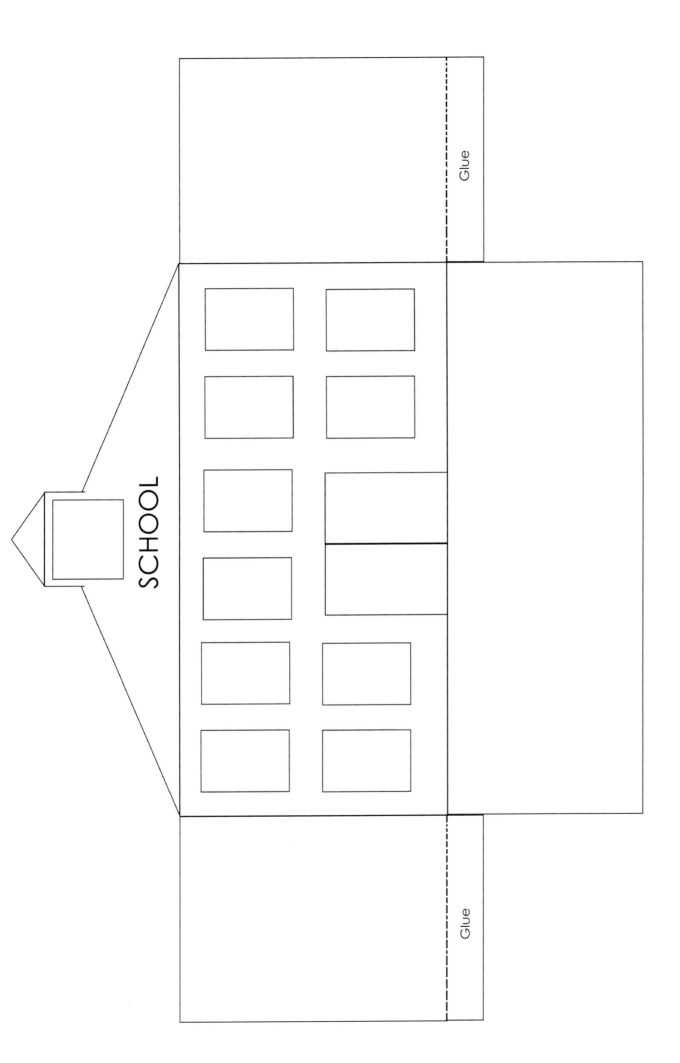

SCHOOL

Glue

Glue

Draw or glue a picture of your state flag here:

I'm from

_____

The _____ state.

I love my state!

State Flower

Write your state motto here:

State Bird

Draw an example of a license plate here:

State Tree

State Seal

State Song

Monarch Butterfly Migration

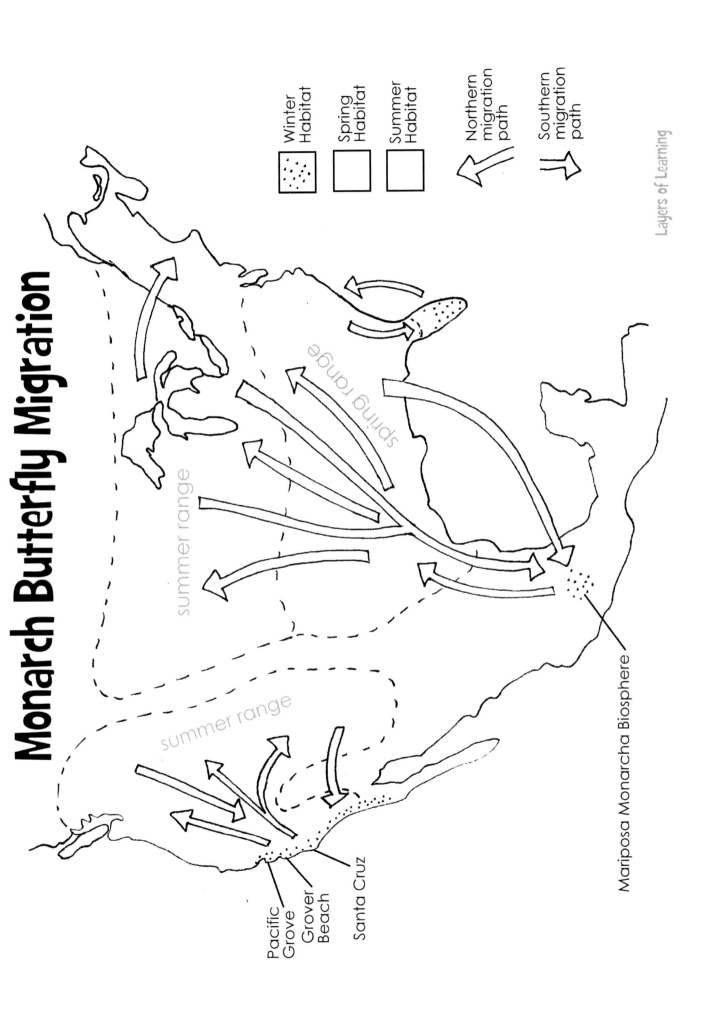

Winter Habitat

Spring Habitat

Summer Habitat

Northern migration path

Southern migration path

spring range

summer range

summer range

Pacific Grove

Grover Beach

Santa Cruz

Mariposa Monarcha Biosphere

Layers of Learning

How Hibernation Works

In the fall . . .

In the winter . . .

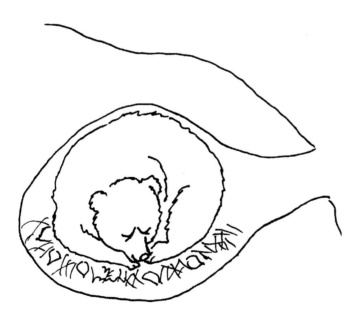

Monarch Butterfly	Viceroy Butterfly	Coral Snake
Foureye Butterflyfish	Transvaal Zebra	Cleaner Wrasse
Red Bird of Paradise	Dead Leaf Butterfly	Chameleon
Bokermannohyla Alvarengai	Granular Poison Arrow Frog	Hoverfly
Skunk	White-tail Deer	Male Crested Partridge

History of the Theater

About the Authors

Karen & Michelle . . .
Mothers, sisters, teachers, women who are passionate
about educating kids.
We are dedicated to lifelong learning.

Karen, a mother of four, who has homeschooled her kids for more than eight years with her husband, Bob, has a bachelor's degree in child development with an emphasis in education. She lives in Idaho, gardens, teaches piano, and plays an excruciating number of board games with her kids. Karen is our resident arts expert and English guru {most necessary as Michelle regularly and carelessly mangles the English language and occasionally steps over the bounds of polite society}.

Michelle and her husband, Cameron, have homeschooled their six boys for more than a decade. Michelle earned a bachelors in biology, making her the resident science expert, though she is mocked by her friends for being the Botanist with the Black Thumb of Death. She also is the go-to for history and government. She believes in staying up late, hot chocolate, and a no whining policy. We both pitch in on geography, in case you were wondering.

Visit our constantly updated blog for tons of free ideas,
free printables, and more cool stuff for sale:
www.Layers-of-Learning.com

Made in the USA
Middletown, DE
04 April 2025

73769526R00031